JOHN CARSON LESTER JR

THE BEST OF THE BEST

That John Carson Lester Jr Has EVER Written on SALES/MARKETING!

PureHeartsInternational.com
Do Well By Doing Good

Copyright © 2018 by John Carson Lester Jr

All rights reserved. No part of this publication may be reproduced, stored or transmitted in any form or by any means, electronic, mechanical, photocopying, recording, scanning, or otherwise without written permission from the publisher. It is illegal to copy this book, post it to a website, or distribute it by any other means without permission.

John Carson Lester Jr asserts the moral right to be identified as the author of this work.

John Carson Lester Jr has no responsibility for the persistence or accuracy of URLs for external or third-party Internet Websites referred to in this publication and does not guarantee that any content on such Websites is, or will remain, accurate or appropriate.

Designations used by companies to distinguish their products are often claimed as trademarks. All brand names and product names used in this book and on its cover are trade names, service marks, trademarks and registered trademarks of their respective owners. The publishers and the book are not associated with any product or vendor mentioned in this book. None of the companies referenced within the book have endorsed the book.

First edition

This book was professionally typeset on Reedsy.
Find out more at reedsy.com

For the "little guy" and "little gal" in the network marketing industry, people I understand and still relate to today despite my decades of substantial achievement in the industry.

"People are not interested in your product or your business; they are interested in solving their own problems." -John Carson Lester Jr

Contents

Foreword	iii
Preface	iv
Acknowledgement	v
Introduction	1
Minimum Pre-Requisites	3
What IS It And What Are People Saying About It?	4
Overview Sayings	6
Step 0 Of 21 Steps	8
Step 1 Of 21 Steps	10
Step 2 Of 21 Steps	11
Step 3 Of 21 Steps	12
Step 4 Of 21 Steps	14
Step 5 Of 21 Steps	16
Step 6 Of 21 Steps	17
Step 7 Of 21 Steps	18
Step 8 Of 21 Steps	19
Step 9 Of 21 Steps	20
Step 10 Of 21 Steps	21
Step 11 Of 21 Steps	23
Step 12 Of 21 Steps	24
Step 13 Of 21 Steps	25
Step 14 Of 21 Steps	27
Step 15 Of 21 Steps	29

Step 16 Of 21 Steps	31
Step 17 Of 21 Steps	32
Step 18 Of 21 Steps	34
Step 19 Of 21 Steps	37
Step 20 Of 21 Steps	46
Step 21 of 21 Steps	48

Foreword

"John Lester's Pied Piper Principles are good. I have known John since the early days of Internet Marketing. In fact, he helped me fight off MLM scam artists on the old AOL MLM Forums. I've subscribed to his newsgroup for years and respect John's marketing wisdom highly. In fact, I have beat him about the head and shoulders to print it in Book format. In fact, I took his CDs and sent the MP3 files to my transcriptionist and am pushing him to get it edited now. WHY? Because it needs to be kept on hand every day as a quick reference on "How To Do Internet Marketing" or any Marketing for that matter. When he gets the book done it will be one of the few books that I sell on my MLM Consumer Protection website." -Rod Cook aka The MLM WatchDog

Preface

I don't just think, I *know* that every "little guy" and "little gal" in the network marketing industry failing over and over again and jumping from one MLM program to another over and over again ad nauseaum to their own great frustration and oftentimes destruction would be able to create success for themselves in any MLM they do as soon as they thoroughly read, comprehend and incorporate the rock-solid and time-proven principles found in my 4 MLM works in this exact order: 1) THE BEST OF THE BEST; 2) PIED PIPER PRINCIPLES; 3) the MLM Screen Pass Tactic; 4) SELF-EMPLOYMENT 101 SERIES; and finally 5) the MLM IGNORANCE TRAP.

Writing from Bacolod City, Negros Occidental in the Philippines on November 22, 2018, John Carson Lester Jr, Owner of MyForbiddenLeads.com

Acknowledgement

As always, I'm both deeply inspired and indebted by the love and for the support I've received in the writing of THE BEST OF THE BEST by the three special women in my life; my fiance Lynlyn Balberde, my sister Jennifer Ann Lester and my mother Armina Virginia Lester; and my late dad, John Carson Lester Sr.

1

Introduction

Hi, Friend. John Carson Lester Jr here. You know, your friendly neighborhood Mentor to the Online Marketing Gurus who in the mid-1990s taught the likes of Jonathan Mizel and Marlon Sanders how to online market (click your "Testimonials - ALL" link at MyForbiddenLeads.com). Your one of only three IRS-registered Founding Members of your Distributor Rights Association. Your DRA Executive Director of Communications. Your DRA Executive Director of Media and Publicity. Owner of the world's only full service MLM genealogy lead list service bureau and full service marketing consulting firm. Your owner of the world's largest full service bulk email company focusing on MLM genealogy lead lists since 1996. Your publisher of not only your THE BEST OF THE BEST but also your PIED PIPER PRINCIPLES, your MLM SCREEN PASS TACTIC, your SELF EMPLOYMENT 101 SERIES and your the MLM IGNORANCE TRAP Amazon Kindle eBooks and Amazon Paperback books. Your May 2005 New Kid on the Block Network Marketing Business Journal

Company. Featured in WIRED. Your $80,000+ in a single month earner. Your transactor w/over 100,000+ people in over 100+ countries around the world. Your 947+ pages of testimonials generator. Your gentleman and a scholar...yatta, yatta, yatta, etc. :)

2

Minimum Pre-Requisites

In order for you to get your maximum benefit out of your THE BEST OF THE BEST purchase, we're assuming that you already have the minimum pre-requisite of deeply understanding that recruiting friends, family and opportunity seekers is the path to your own MLM destruction and that only recruiting real network marketers is the path to your own MLM success. For the necessary background info on this topic, simply click on your appropriate FAQs links near the very top of http://www.MyForbiddenLeads.com and read and learn.

3

What IS It And What Are People Saying About It?

THE BEST OF THE BEST is a gemSTARS-R-NICErs homebizAUTOMATED.com CLASSIC of CLASSICS! It was originally written back in 1997 after compiling several years worth of other notes.

Here's what John Vasey, a past student of gemSTARS-R-NICErs, who has gone on to earn literally hundreds and hundreds of thousands of dollars with a well known financial services multi-affiliate marketing company, had to say about "The Best of the Best" in a testimonial he wrote over one of our gemSTARS-R-NICErs global email discussion lists in September of 1999:

"I've spent 3 years studying Nicers and in the next rolling year I'm on track to earn a million dollars, crazy but true. Study, internalize the emails John Lester sent the other day The best I have ever written on sales and Marketing-They are absolutely priceless. Nicers has taught me more about sales and marketing than *any* course that I paid hundreds sometime thousands. John Lester is one of my all time heroes in life not just in sales and marketing but the values he teaches we will keep forever and you will hear the same testimony from the other *old timers* such as

Tim, Peggy Hendricks etc Participating in the Nicers community is the greatest single thing I have ever done professionally. I say when you mention Nicers we literally should all bow our virtual heads." -John Vasey

4

Overview Sayings

* repetition is the mother of all skill
* practice does not make perfect; practice makes PERMANENT
* massive action solves ALL PROBLEMS
* you have to work more on YOU than the product/service you sell
* your Daily Method of Operation is more important than your marketing plan or products
* you're always moving in the current direction of your current thoughts
* can't fix conversation; can only fix experience
* what you start with is what you end with...start w/ strength, you end w/strength, start w/weakness, you end w/weakness
* speed of the leader, speed of the pack
* atttitude breeds activity
* adversity is designed for growth
* in life you cannot prosper more than what you have the CAPACITY to handle!

* the prosperity test will be far greater than the adversity test
* adversity and struggles are inevitable; stress is OPTIONAL
* if it isn't necessary to say, it's necessary NOT to say
* we ALL have the gift of communication; DEVELOP the RARE gift of ENCOURAGEMENT as the marketplace values it GREATLY
* you can't SEE momentum; you can only FEEL momentum
* advancement of momentum is AUTOMATIC w/daily application of your DMO (daily method of operation)
* your life is a mental attitude
* what we are after is RELAXED intensity
* emotions can't think and they are not sustainable for the salesperson
* key to success: measurable amount of progress in a reasonable amount of time
* inch by inch is a cinch; yard by yard is hard
* consistency and persistency eliminates all barriers
* this is a speed of exposure business
* this business is about PEOPLE-MOMENTUM-VOLUME-CHECKS
* personal development always comes before the fortune
* an IMPERFECT plan started TODAY is better than a PERFECT plan started next week; because "perfect" doesn't exist and "next week" never comes
* don't focus on what you DON'T have; focus on what you DO have
* you build a business the same way you build a life or a house; one day at a time, one brick at a time
* the fortune is in the followup!

5

Step 0 Of 21 Steps

****21 STEPS to Sales/Marketing Success! gemSTARS-R-NICErs STYLE!****

0) Read John Carson Lester Jr's Self Employment 101 Series of 18 comprehensive lessons as it teaches you how to "Self Employ Yourself" and you *probably* have *no clue* as to how to *really* SELF EMPLOY YOURSELF! John Carson Lester Jr certainly didn't know how to self employ himself when he started his journey of self employment back in 1990, despite the fact that he had been a straight commission salesperson for the previous 5 years, the closest thing to being "self employed" as there is without actually being self-employed. He had worked inside large companies from 1985 thru 1989 and was provided with all the things that large companies provide that people take for granted until they are out on their own 100%. He discovered the dramatic difference between being on 100% commission inside of a large, well-established company and trying to get a homebiz off the ground when you're sitting at home 100% on your own. He discovered that contrary to what he had previously thought, that self employment was going to be a cinch, that there is an entirely different SKILL SET required to be successfully self employed compared to the SKILL SET required to be an employee (even a 100% straight commission employee)! Successful homebiz self employment is NOT an easy thing to accomplish unless you have a SYSTEM like gemSTARS-R-NICErs homebizAUTOMATED.com SYSTEMS on your side! Why? because it has the SELF EMPLOYMENT SKILL SET and TBOTB built...INSIDE! :)

6

Step 1 Of 21 Steps

1) We understand that we do *not* get paid for making sales!

7

Step 2 Of 21 Steps

2) We understand that we get *paid* for communicating with people (Activity) and SORTING (more on SORTING below) and leading the remaining non-SORTED BELLY to BELLY (more on BELLY to BELLY below) prospects to DECISIONS! We get paid for obtaining DECISIONS no matter WHAT that decision happens to be, Yes or No (Maybes not allowed)!

8

Step 3 Of 21 Steps

3) We understand that we get paid EXACTLY the SAME for a "no" DECISION from a SORTED BELLY to BELLY prospect as we do a "yes" DECISION from a SORTED BELLY to BELLY prospect! That's correct. We do *not* get paid for making sales! Sales are a RESULT! A result of *communicating* with people and SORTING and leading them BELLY to BELLY to DECISIONS!

STORY: Door-to-door salesperson sits down with his boss, frustrated that he's not making as many sales as he would like. Boss says, "'Bob' (let's call him Bob), the problem is, you don't understand how you get paid! You THINK, Bob, that you get paid for making sales. But that's NOT how you get paid, Bob. Sales are a RESULT! Let me explain," says the boss. "Have you kept track of your numbers, Bob? How many presentations do you have to make to get a sale?"

Bob answers, "three."

Boss asks, "And how many doors do you have to knock on before you get three presentations?"

Bob answers, "ten."

Boss asks, "And how much do we pay you, Bob, for every sale?"

Bob answers, "$100."

Boss replies, "YOUR PROBLEM, Bob, is that you are dividing $100 by ONE SALE; you need to be dividing $100 by TEN DOORS. You DON'T MAKE $100 for every sale, Bob, you make $10 for EVERY DOOR you knock on, REGARDLESS of what they say, whether they give you a presentation, are rude to you, whatever! THE NOs don't control your financial future, Bob! The NUMBER OF DOORS ~YOU~ knock on controls YOUR financial future! You make $10 FOR EVERY DOOR YOU KNOCK ON NO MATTER WHAT THEY SAY AND NO MATTER WHAT HAPPENS!"

Bob SUDDENLY gets up and starts to leave the boss' office. Boss says, "Whoa, Bob, what's wrong, did I offend you or something?" Bob says, "No boss, but I gotta run! ***DO YOU KNOW HOW MANY DOORS THERE ARE IN THIS TOWN?!***"

9

Step 4 Of 21 Steps

4) We understand that we shake "No" decisions from our "sandals."

STORY: a long, long time ago, a GREAT LEADER (in my opinion, the GREATEST LEADER) sent out 12 "frontliners" to spread a great, great message. But before they went out, they were warned by their Leader that anyplace that did not RECEIVE their message, before they moved on to the next place, to SHAKE OUT THE SAND FROM THEIR SANDALS as a testimony AGAINST that place.

What could that have meant?

Well, it probably means several things but one thing that it means is, hey, one grain of sand in the shoe probably won't bother you too much, just be mildly irritating. But get SEVERAL grains of sands in your shoe and you can get a blister. And a blister could get infected. And you could lose YOUR FOOT. And if you lose your foot, you could lose YOUR LIFE!

Therefore, it's NOT IMPORTANT that "they" buy any part of YOUR STORY—your JOB is to simply TELL IT to as many people as you can every day and get as many Yes or No DECISIONS that you can—what's MOST IMPORTANT to YOU is that YOU don't buy any part of "THEIR MESSAGE!" Especially if it is a "No" decision!

Remember, we get paid EXACTLY the same for a "No" decision as a "Yes" DECISION simply because we simply get paid for communicating with people and getting DECISIONS. When you get a "No" decision, don't "buy" into ANY part of the reasons they give for their "No" decision. Just shake the sand of their "No" decision out of your sandals and leave the town of their "No" decision and move on to the next town of your next DECISION!

10

Step 5 Of 21 Steps

5) We understand that if we talk to NO people and get NO decisions, we make NO money!

11

Step 6 Of 21 Steps

6) We understand that if we talk to SOME people and get SOME decisions, we make SOME money!

12

Step 7 Of 21 Steps

7) We understand that if we talk to LOTS of people, and get LOTS of decisions, we make LOTS of money!

13

Step 8 Of 21 Steps

8) We understand that we get our DECISIONS *quickly* because this is called PROSPECTING! After all, amateurs CONVINCE, but pros SORT! That's what sales and marketing is all about, SORTING through large numbers of people as quickly as possible, kind of like the goldminers of 1849 used to PROSPECT for gold. They would sift very, very fast. The FASTEST sifters were the ones that did the best and found the most gold.

14

Step 9 Of 21 Steps

9) We understand that our teasers and pitches are not DECISION obtaining tools, they are SORTING tools. Therefore, *NO* teaser and/or pitch ALONE will, by itself, make a career level income for you. You almost never close during the SORTING phase of sending teaser and pitches; you only close during the BELLY to BELLY phase (AGAIN, more on BELLY to BELLY below). *Closing* thru obtaining *decisions* is where virtually *all* the money happens to be.

15

Step 10 Of 21 Steps

10) We understand that it is foolish to spend much time agonizing over "is my teaser good enough, is my pitch good enough?" Secret: you CAN'T say the WRONG thing to the RIGHT person! Secret: you CAN'T say the RIGHT thing to the WRONG person! And, An imperfect plan STARTED today, is BETTER! than a "perfect" plan started "next week," because "perfect" *doesn't* exist and "next week" *never* arrives. Just PITCH! PITCH! PITCH! and TALK TO PEOPLE! TALK TO PEOPLE! TALK TO PEOPLE! and GET DECISIONS! GET DECISIONS! and GET DECISIONS! and you WILL then FIND that MASSIVE ACTION really DOES SOLVE ALL PROBLEMS.<g>

STORY: What happens when you drop an inexperienced salesperson from a helicopter (with a parachute, of course...<g>) onto Times Square with an index card with the following 2 pitches written: "You wouldn't want to buy my products, would you?" and "You wouldn't want to try my opportunity, would you?" and s/he pitches that 8 hours a day in the middle of Times Square with thousands of people hustling and bustling by? What happens? Answer: several times per hour, somebodies are going to stop and say, "I dunno. Whatcha got?" and then that salesperson has an opportunity to start getting BELLY to BELLY because the teaser has done its SORTING job.

Your teaser and pitch doesn't really matter; what matters is that you PITCH them to start the SORTING PROCESS so that you can GET to DECISIONS where we get paid! MASSIVE ACTIONS *really does* solve! ALL! problems!

16

Step 11 Of 21 Steps

11) We understand that we have to communicate with NEW people every day through our D.M.O. D.aily M.ethod of O.peration (Activity)!

17

Step 12 Of 21 Steps

12) We understand that we have *safety* in numbers and a law of averages! S.I.N.A.L.O.A. is an acronym for S.afety I.n N.umbers A.nd L.aw O.f A.verages. What this means is that any Daily Method of Operation that you establish to communicate your marketing messages to LOTS OF NEW PEOPLE is going to have a S.I.N.A.L.O.A. attached to it. It might be 1 in 2 people; it might be 1 in 10 people; in might be 2 in 100 people; BUT, whatever it is, you can always, as long as you keep sending out your marketing messages through whatever media you are using (telemarketing, direct mail, email, face to face, whatever), you are going to always end up averaging your SINALOA for that particular Daily Method of Operation. And so there is SAFETY in SINALOA in DOING it; conversely, there is DANGER in NOT doing your DMO in order to put SINALOA in YOUR FAVOR.

So the choice is up to every individual entrepreneur; am I going to plug SAFETY into my business, or am I going to plug DANGER into my business?

18

Step 13 Of 21 Steps

13) We understand that we have a PIPELINE that we must fill through daily application of our D.M.O (D.aily M.ethod of O.peration)!

PIPELINE says although I get paid IMMEDIATELY as soon as I begin talking to people, I won't actually SEE the checks for a few weeks or months down the road, but if I want to truly see those checks, I have to just put my head down and CONSISTENTLY talk to people, work my DMO, build up momentum and fill up that pipeline!

You can always count on PIPELINE to work either IN YOUR FAVOR or AGAINST YOU, depending on whether YOU are FILLING YOUR PIPELINE or NOT. An example of a NICErsPRO reseller's DMO is Kim Carrig's and Gary DuVall's DMO of contacting people at WWW classified ad sites and sending teasers to those people and sending pitches to the positive respondents and then getting Belly to Belly. So, Kim and Gary ESTABLISH MOMENTUM by contacting these sources and they consistently solicit new people and follow up with their old leads as well!

Think of PIPELINE as a PIPELINE. And you're the one who fills it up with water (MARKETING MESSAGES...that YOU generate about your products and services). But this PIPELINE is like any other PIPELINE. It's not some short stubby thing. It's a *long* PIPELINE like any other PIPELINE.

Question: if someone poured just ONE glass of water (MARKETING MESSAGES) just ONE time in a long, skinny PIPELINE, would it be REALISTIC to expect a torrent of water to come gushing out continuously on the other end? Of course not.<g>

And yet that's exactly what so many inexperienced marketers (and some that THINK they are experienced but are not) do all the time. They pour a little bit of water into the PIPELINE, one time, then they RUN to the other side and scratch their head in bewilderment and frustration when there isn't a torrent of continuously gushing water (SALES) coming out the other end!

Unrealistic expectations.

Here's what PIPELINE is ALL ABOUT: as marketers, we HAVE to understand that WHAT we DO TODAY doesn't show up until TOMORROW!

WHAT we DO THIS WEEK doesn't show up until NEXT WEEK!

WHAT we DO THIS MONTH doesn't show up until NEXT MONTH!

WHAT we DO THIS QUARTER doesn't show up until NEXT QUARTER!

WHAT we DO THIS YEAR doesn't show up until NEXT YEAR!

WHAT we DO THIS DECADE doesn't show up until NEXT DECADE!

WHAT we do THIS LIFE doesn't show up until THE NEXT LIFE!

19

Step 14 Of 21 Steps

14) We understand that the PIPELINE is also a PRODUCTION LINE! also known as the *sales process.*

Note: see the automobile PRODUCTION LINE picture in YOUR MAP! under #1 YOUR SYSTEM!

Just as the PIPELINE must be continuously filled with new TEASER communications being sent out, the PIPELINE is ALSO a PRODUCTION LINE where, in different STAGES of the PIPELINE-PRODUCTION LINE SORTING! is occuring so that the FINAL STAGE of the PIPELINE-PRODUCTION LINE is BELLY to BELLY contact designed to obtain DECISIONS!

There will be far fewer BELLY to BELLY decisions coming out of the END of the PIPELINE-PRODUCTION LINE than there were TEASERS poured into the BEGINNING of the PIPELINE-PRODUCTION LINE.

It takes *time* to move people through the SORTING-DECISION MAKING PROCESS (both the prospects *and* yourself are making SORTING DECISIONS along the way), which is why we say with regards to the PIPELINE-PRODUCTION LINE:

WHAT we DO TODAY doesn't show up until TOMORROW!

WHAT we DO THIS WEEK doesn't show up until NEXT WEEK!

WHAT we DO THIS MONTH doesn't show up until NEXT MONTH!

WHAT we DO THIS QUARTER doesn't show up until NEXT QUARTER!

WHAT we DO THIS YEAR doesn't show up until NEXT YEAR!

WHAT we DO THIS DECADE doesn't show up until NEXT DECADE!

WHAT we do THIS LIFE doesn't show up until THE NEXT LIFE!

20

Step 15 Of 21 Steps

15) We understand that we must establish, sustain, and advance MOMENTUM through CONSISTENCY of application of our DMO! Establishing, sustaining and advancing MOMENTUM all comes down to the CONSISTENCY FACTOR. The way to get that PIPELINE POURING OUT WATER ON THE OTHER END (sales) is to CONSISTENTLY be POURING MARKETING MESSAGES into the TOP of that PIPELINE. And by consistently, I mean CONSISTENTLY, whatever DMO you set up, to keep at IT and keep at it. Sooner or later (and sooner the more consistent you are), you'll have success HUNTING you down.

You ESTABLISH momentum by doing your DMO 2! that's 2! repeat, that's 2! times!

How do you then SUSTAIN momentum? By doing your DMO again!

How do you ADVANCE momentum? By doing your DMO again! and again! and again!

The equation is, PEOPLE-MOMENTUM-VOLUME-CHECKS!

You get PEOPLE by TALKING TO LOTS OF PEOPLE.

You get MOMENTUM by producing LOTS OF PEOPLE and then

SUPPORTING those people.

MOMENTUM produces VOLUME and VOLUME produces CHECKS!

You CANNOT get the RESULT! of SALES without the CAUSE! of PROLONGED PERIODS OF CONSISTENT ACTIVITY thru CONSISTENT APPLICATION OF YOUR DMO!

21

Step 16 Of 21 Steps

16) We understand that *consistently applying* SINALOA, PIPELINE-PRODUCTION LINE and MOMENTUM means that our *pay* per *unit* of time is *always increasing* just like *compound interest.* See, when we say there is a SINALOA in your direct email, that MEANS that there is a MONETARY VALUE based on YOUR consistency, your skill levels, your followup skills, etc, on EVERY teaser that you send out, every pitch that you send out, every followup that you do, every BELLY to BELLY decision that you obtain, etc.

Let's say that it starts out as a PENNY per contact. How many pennies do you want to make? Send that number of contacts. But with consistency of EFFORT, just like MUSCLE BUILDING, pretty soon, your EFFORTS may be YIELDING bigger muscles, like a nickel per contact, eventually, maybe a quarter per email, eventually, maybe $20 per contact, as COMPOUND INTEREST begins to kick in in terms of success breeding success. Stop and think about that one a bit. The success breeding success part, that is.

22

Step 17 Of 21 Steps

17) We understand that we CANNOT be FOCUSED on OUR NEEDS, OUR SURVIVAL, the $ that WE NEED to make it, pay the rent, buy groceries, etc, etc, etc.

We understand that we HAVE to be FOCUSED on our PROSPECT's NEEDS and the WAY for THAT to happen is to HAVE A CAUSE BIGGER THAN OURSELVES!

We understand that the only way to keep ourselves motivated in the long term is to have a HIGHER PURPOSE than just our own selfish needs.

As soon as we do the above, along with stopping worrying about whether we "make a sale" or not for OURSELVES, and START focusing on HELPING to create another SUCCESS STORY out of your prospect's life or business, THAT is when we will start enjoying SUCCESS!

SUCCESS...it's an INSIDE job. That's where it all starts and ends!

And of course, we understand that when the "sale" is made ("yes" DECISION), the REAL SALE has JUST BEGUN.<g>

So don't get excited about SALES, consider yourself an AMBAS-

SADOR of your products and services looking to benefit a new country that you want to establish excellent diplomatic relations with (your prospect) and you'll be JUST FINE no matter what any SINGLE individual SAYS, good, bad, or indifferent.

And by being a hard working, industrious AMBASSADOR that has created for himself/herself SO MANY opportunities to establish relations with SO MANY countries, you'll NEVER put pressure on any single country to establish relations, and thereby, paradoxically, end up having MANY MORE nations *want* to establish relations with YOU as a result.

23

Step 18 Of 21 Steps

18) We understand that if we come off sounding like a salesperson, we lose.

EVERYONE in life is FIGHTING THE WAR of life!

If you come off sounding like someone who is going to HELP THEM FIGHT *THEIR* WARS (and everybody's *wars* are *different* although there are many similar *battles*), then you will win the highest percentage of the time that you could possibly win.

Which is the best that you could possibly do, which is what you want.

Why is that? Why is this approach the best way to get people COMMUNICATING WITH YOU?

Well, think of the following picture that hangs in sales offices across the nation! BACKGROUND: medieval war, soldiers on two opposing sides fighting on horses, using swords, bows and arrrows, and other primitive weapons. FOREGROUND: tent, with a salesperson on one side, arms crossed, legs crossed, looking very cocky and confident, standing next to a machine gun! On the other side of the tent is a General whose gaze is fixed on the war proceeding on the battlefield, and a Junior Officer trying to get the General's attention by stating, "General, there is a salesperson here to see you!" The General cannot see the salesperson because the salesperson is out of sight on the other side of the tent, and besides, his gaze is fixed on the battlefield, and he replies to the Junior Officer, irritably, "I don't have any time to see a SALESPERSON! Can't you see that I am fighting a WAR here!"

Most of you fail in your marketing efforts because your MESSAGE (the Junior Officer), is WRONG! You broadcast, in so many ways, rather, you EMOTIONALLY PROJECT, THAT YOU ARE JUST TRYING to SELL SOMETHING to the other person!

Guess what?

The OTHER PERSON doesn't want to buy your stuff!

Why? Because s/he is SO CONSUMED, SO DISTRACTED, STRUGGLING trying to WIN THEIR WARS OF LIFE, that if you approach them sounding like a SALESPERSON, they are not going to remove their eyes from their BATTLEFIELD and they will NEVER *see* your MACHINE GUN (NICErsPRO, NICErs, etc)!

You're *just* a DISTRACTION! of their attention! from THEIR WAR! if you're viewed as being "just" a salesperson!

THEY DON'T WANT TO BUY YOUR STUFF! BUT THEY *DO* WANT TO WIN THEIR WAR! SO YOUR JOB IS TO GET THEIR ATTENTION AND THE WAY YOU GET THEIR ATTENTION IS TO FOCUS THEIR FOCUS ON THE FACT THAT YOU'RE THERE TO HELP THEM WIN THEIR WAR!

Now, wouldn't things have been different IF, INSTEAD of telling the Junior Officer that a SALESPERSON was here to see the General, if that salesperson told the Junior Officer (the messenger), that there was a person to see the General that had a piece of war equipment that would VANQUISH the entire army of the enemy in mere seconds?!

Do you think THAT MESSAGE would have GOT THE GENERAL'S ATTENTION?!

You bet it would!

The POWER OF WORDS can never be underestimated in the world of sales/marketing!

LITTLE THINGS make ALL THE DIFFERENCE IN THE WORLD!

You need to IMMEDIATELY, at the BEGINNING of the contact, come off sounding like you are interested in helping this person FIGHT THEIR WAR! NOT YOURS!

24

Step 19 Of 21 Steps

19) We understand that we transition from PITCH to BELLY to BELLY by drawing the prospect's EYES from viewing the BATTLEFIELD of THEIR WARS OF LIFE by SHOCKING THEM by sounding UNLIKE ANY SALESPERSON they have ever encountered before!

And that is accomplished by starting the BELLY to BELLY process by initiating the 3-step closing method. The way you do the 3-step closing method is DIFFERENT depending on whether you are retailing a product/service or whether you are in a RECRUITING situation.

Here's the retailing approach first. Step 1: Ask them WHAT THEY WANT with CPS (Confidence, Pride and Service). Example: Mr. Prospect, tell me WHAT YOU WANT! number it even! list it right out for us because, after all, we're NICErs (Confidence)! the world's ONLY! Bulk Email University (Pride)! and we'll GET THE JOB DONE FOR YOU! We'll take care of ya! (Service)

After you wake them up from their fainting spell, having never been approached by a salesperson in that manner, since nearly all salespeople have no idea what they are doing, and now that they are RELAXED because they *know* that they are in good hands with a PRO, go to:

Step 2. Now that they have LISTED for you the WARS OF THEIR LIFE, more income, more time with family, more creative control over career, more career satisfaction, etc. you ask CLOSING QUESTIONS directly derived from THEIR WARS indicating that you have NOT ONLY LISTENED (caring) but that you HAVE the MACHINE GUNS that THEY NEED to FIGHT THEIR WARS! (feature) and that winning their war will allow them to return home to their LOVING, HAPPY SPOUSES THAT THEY HAVEN'T SEEN IN SO LONG! (emotionless feature translated into emotional benefit)

Example on how to fight the war of becoming successfully self- employed. Mr. Prospect, seeing that you want to learn how to become self-employed, do ya think it would be a good idea to become associated with Bulk Email University? Answer: Yes. (feature) Mr. Prospect, seeing that you want to learn how to become self-employed, do ya think that it would be a good idea to become associated with Bulk Email University where you have hundreds and thousands of teachers that are ALREADY successfully self- employed? (extended feature) Mr. Prospect, seeing that you want to learn how to become self-employed, do ya think that it would be a good idea to become associated with Bulk Email University where you have hundreds and thousands of teachers that are ALREADY successfully self-employed where you can finally enjoy the good life of being able to spend more time with your loving family instead of bowing down to the corporate God that you despise and hate so terribly? (emotionless feature translated into emotional benefit)

UNDERVIEW: And then, as part of Step # 2, you go through this "Do ya think it would be a good idea..." for every WAR they have listed that they want to fight and win. Every one of them and it's important that you start each sentence off just the way that it is listed above...Mr./Ms. Prospect, seeing that you want...do ya think it would be a good idea...

S/he that controls the QUESTIONS, controls the ANSWERS. You should be getting numerous YESES along the way here. The more YESES you get here, the more LIKELY you'll get a yes in Step 3.

Step 3: Mr. Prospect, WHAT DO YOU THINK YA OUGHTA DO?! Shut up.

You want the Prospect to speak first now. And *respect* their decision. Remember, amateurs CONVINCE, pros SORT. Thank them for the money for their DECISION, regardless of what it is, and if it's a NO, then move on, if it is a YES, remember, the SALE has just begun...

Now, if you are RECRUITING, here's a clip from an email note that explains how it is SLIGHTLY different.

How to close! is something that most FULL TIME salespeople do not know how to do!

When you're recruiting for a network marketing program, here's what you do: 1. After introducing yourself, ask QUESTIONS. LOTS of Questions. Start off by asking them if they currently have a job or not. Your subtle psychological positioning in this phone call or email correspondence (phone calls are better but you can do this thru email as well) is basically: look, you answered my ad, you're obviously dissatisfied with something and are looking, you're the interviewee and I'm the interviewer.

But that has to be communicated in a very subtle psychological way or they'll reject the control you're attempting to establish. It will take some practice to get good at this.

The reasons why you ask them about their job are several

fold: You want to get an idea as to whether they can afford what you are offering. But more importantly, you want them to talk about something they are UNHAPPY about, INSECURE about and DISSATISFIED with at the present time. And that is their JOB or their current occupation field which they probably are unhappy with to some degree or another otherwise why would they be looking for a home-based business?

The reason why you want them to start talking about their job, frankly, is so that they talk about something they feel INSECURE about (most people feel insecure about their jobs and their place in the world, etc) to help you, in a very subtle manner, gain the upper hand where they slip down the slippery slope (without even realizing it) of having to prove to YOU as the MIGHTY FOUNDER of the gemSTARS-R-NICErs SYSTEMS their worthiness to do business with YOU!

If they slip down the slippery road of having to justify a job they aren't happy with, you're halfway home towards establishing that quiet control that you want to establish.

ABOVE ALL, SAY ALMOST NOTHING. Ask the questions. Let them then talk. NATURE ABHORS A VACUUM. Let them fill the vacuum. Then as they start talking about their current job and occupational background and experience, their insecurities will start to show, typically, without you even saying a word and oftentimes they'll start pressing in an attempt to impress you. It's a natural thing to start doing if you're the only one talking and you're talking about your own occupational background, achievements, education, etc. that you happen to feel INSECURE about anyways!

So first you INTRODUCE yourself, and here's how:

Hi, this is Your Name, Founder of gemSTARS-R-NICErs. Is this Prospect Name? Congratulations Prospect Name! Congratulations for answering my Internet ad, the purple web page, gemSTARS-R-NICErs, etc. Obviously you're seeking something FirstName...so tell me, FirstName... Do you have a job? what's your current occupation? why are you looking into having a home-based business? Do you have $XXX to invest in your business? what's your current level of education? have you ever managed people before? do you like people? do you work well with people? have you ever owned and operated your own business before?

Those questions immediately above are what I call the "insecurity" help you establish control questions that we described in great detail above.

If you hear them bring up a "fear of loss" issue in their answers, jump all over that like a hungry dog on a meaty bone! For example, if they mentioned generally that one of the reasons that they are looking into a home-based business is because of all the layoffs happening in the corporate world, ask them "Is the reason why you're afraid of corporate layoffs is because you've been laid off before?" because if their answer is yes, all of that FEAR OF LOSS emotion will rush all over them again right there on that phone call. And there are TWO (2) powerful buttons to push in any selling situation, FEAR OF LOSS and GREED of GAIN and of the two buttons, FEAR OF LOSS is always more powerful than the very powerful GREED of GAIN. But it's always better to let them TALK ABOUT their fear of loss situation, so ask them, "How did it FEEL when you got that layoff notice?"

Now we move on to the "GREED OF GAIN" part of the questioning: why are you interested in a HOME-based business vs a Main Street non-home-based business? What attracted you to the X multi-affiliate marketing program specifically? What attracted you to gemSTARS-R-NICErs specifically? Now, here, the length and quality and content quality of their answers will largely depend on how much of our sales letters/self-replicated web pages they have previously absorbed prior to your phone or email contact. Do not help them answer these questions unless their answers are very short in this area, particularly to the X multi-affiliate question and the gemSTARS-R-NICErs question.

If you do need to help them out in the X multi-affiliate program/gemSTARS-R-NICErs area, you ask them questions that go like this, and they ALWAYS start out with this formula..."Well, NAME, doya think it would be a good idea to associate yourself with a group like gemSTARS-R-NICErs that will do this for you..." and then I tailor the THIS to *push* the "hot buttons" that they've revealed to me throughout the course of the questioning (want to spend more time with spouse, make more money, spend more time with children, establish a retirement fund, establish a college fund, whatever). Remember, I wrote all of those things down on a piece of paper, index card, something, as they provided me with that incredibly valuable information about themselves.

At this point, if you're helping them with their answer to the X multi-affiliate program and/or gemSTARS-R-NICErs questions in the 2nd section, OR sometimes, after they've gone thru the insecure thing I describe above as they talk about THEIR occupational accomplishments, then they will "recover" a little bit in the midst of "slipping down the slippery slope of INsecurity about their occupational situation and/or life in general" and ask you, well, tell me a little bit about you?

That's when YOU say: 1) "gemSTARS-R-NICErs (John Carson Lester Jr) received a phone call from a Wired reporter in December of 1996 and was interviewed and quoted in a January 1997 feature article on the web by WIRED magazine for being an online home-based business pioneer FIRSTNAME! doya think it would be a good idea to associate yourself with that kinda group (person) FirstName?" Wait for their answer, it's typically yes, especially once you've practiced this a few times or more.

2) "gemSTARS-R-NICErs (John Carson Lester Jr) is known as THE "Mentor to the Online Marketing Gurus" do ya think it would be a good idea to associate yourself with that kinda group (person) FirstName?" Wait for their answer, it's typically yes, especially once you've practiced this a few times or more.

3) "gemSTARS-R-NICErs (John Carson Lester Jr) has 947 pages of glowing testimonials from ordinary people it's (he's) helped in 100+ countries around the world. do ya think it would be a good idea to associate yourself with that kinda group (person) FirstName?" Wait for their answer, it's typically yes, especially once you've practiced this a few times or more.

4) "gemSTARS-R-NICErs (John Carson Lester Jr) has made well over $2 million out of its (his) homebased businesses over the past 5 years. Doya think it would be a good idea to associate yourself with that kinda group (person) FirstName?" Wait for their answer, it's typically yes, especially once you've practiced this a few times or more.

Note: by the way, don't number the questions for the prospect, K?<g>

THEN: "Hmmm, well, NAME, I think gemSTARS-R-NICErs (John Carson Lester Jr) is willing to take a chance on you - will that be MasterCard, Visa, American Express or Discover?

You memorize those four questions above and if and when it comes up, you REPACKAGE the four points above using the formula above, ask it in kind of a low-keyed way kind of like it's no big deal..."Well, NAME, doya think it would be a good idea to associate yourself with a group (person) like gemSTARS-R-

NICErs (John Carson Lester Jr) that was written up in a feature article on the web by WIRED magazine in January of 1997....?" and then go on to questions 2, 3 and 4 above using the EXACT same FORMULA.

Now, here, you do NOT REALLY ASK for the order as you read the words in the closing question above where you ask for the plastic! You just flat out ASSUME the order! And the way you do it, just as if you were the INTERVIEWER in a job interview with an EAGER applicant in front of you across the desk trying to prove themselves to you, what you do is, at the end, say, kind of with some hesitation like you're not 100% certain, "Hmmm, well, NAME, I think we're willing to take a chance on you...will that be MasterCard, Visa American Express or Discover?"

Make sure your voice goes UP on the last syllable of Discover as when the last syllable in a sentence goes DOWN, that's a LACK of expectation; flat means neutral expectations; and UP means POSITIVE expectations! It's part of the non-verbal emotional communication that occurs on a phone call!

Remember, the self-replicating web pages really DO put you in the POSITION as the MIGHTY FOUNDER of gemSTARS-R-NICErs to have YOUR PROSPECTS trying to PROVE TO YOU that they are a "worthy" prospect if you ASSUME THE MANTLE and PYSCHOLOGICALLY PUT YOURSELF IN YOUR MIND as BEing the MIGHTY FOUNDER of gemSTARS-R-NICErs! The self-replicating web pages really do put EVERY ONE OF YOU in that kind of a position if you'll absorb this teaching and learn how to leverage yourself off of it. If they reject your gracious OPPORTUNITY OFFER when you weren't even certain whether they were even WORTHY of it, then dust off your sandals and move on to the NEXT TOWN and the NEXT! EAGER APPLICANT!

MEMORIZE The Best of the Best. It will make you a millionaire.

It has many other people...already. And there's more of them to come. :)

25

Step 20 Of 21 Steps

20) We understand that we need to do # 19 at least 20 times per day. In order to be successful sales/marketers, we *have* to get 20 BELLY TO BELLY DECISIONS, be they yeses or noes, it does not matter, but we *have* to get 20 DECISIONS per day in order to be successful.

Therefore, we need to have 20 pennies by our computer every day. You have to start off with something like this: 1000 contacts a day to get 187 pitch requests, then turn around and email a followup letter to ALL 1000 again asking them about their opportunities (like waving a red cape in front of a bull) to draw *even more* out of their shell communicating with you, and remind them that you emailed them the other day. Now you get about 50 or so people emailing you back and forth and you get BELLY to BELLY with them as per # 19, get your 20 DECISIONS *for that day,* and you KEEP FILLING UP THE PIPELINE WITH NEW CONTACTS so that you are CONSTANTLY DOING THIS WITH NEW PEOPLE so that you can be ABCing (Always Be Closing), so that you CONSTANTLY have AT LEAST 20 people a day that you HAVE PROPERLY WORKED INTO THE

STEP 20 OF 21 STEPS

RIGHT POSITION (according to the directions above), where you are JUSTIFIED and asking at THE RIGHT TIME the CLOSING QUESTION more or less in the manner that I indicated above and by getting 20 DECISIONS a day, you'll end up getting 1-2 or sometimes more sales per day!

The rest will be noes.

But you will be PAID EXACTLY THE SAME FOR A YES AS A NO since you KNOW that you get paid for getting DECISIONS asked at the right point of the sales process and that the HIGHEST PAID PERSON is the person that gets the MOST DECISIONS (most of which will always be No).

Put 20 pennies by your computer every day and do not stop putting out teasers until at the end of the day you can honestly be able to move those 20 pennies to the other side of the computer after working them to the right point in the sales process and asking those 20 people the CLOSING QUESTION: Well, whadya think ya oughta do?!

Secret of ALL SALES SUCCESS as given to me by my first sales manager: STPBTBED. S.ee T.wenty P.eople B.elly T.o B.elly E.very D.ay!!!

26

Step 21 of 21 Steps

21) We understand that all of the above is simply known as THE LAW OF SOWING AND REAPING! Every day every sales/marketer PROVES it EITHER in the affirmative or the negative based on their ACTIVITY LEVEL! and their understanding of all of the above as measured by their RESULTS and THEIR BANK ACCOUNTS!

Know that the above is either working FOR YOU or working AGAINST YOU.

It is NEVER NEUTRAL.

When I share this sales/marketing wisdom with many people, especially with the folks that I call "sales hacks" (I was one once too), I get folks nodding their heads all the time, uh-huh, sure, I know that, that's simple, everybody in marketing knows that, that's basic stuff.

Well, apparently it is NOT BASIC stuff since ALOT of people in marketing demonstrate by their ACTIONS or INACTIONS that they DON'T understand these three powerful principles.

And through the size of their bank accounts too.

If you're marketing correctly and treating people correctly

and creating VALUE for people, then your bank accounts will REFLECT that fact.

For things to change, WE have to CHANGE!

For things to get better, WE have to get BETTER!

You're welcome!

The End.

www.ingramcontent.com/pod-product-compliance
Lightning Source LLC
Chambersburg PA
CBHW031531210526
45463CB00010B/2710